SIMPSONS™
COMICS

JAM-PACKED JAMBOREE

TITAN BOOKS

SIMPSONS COMICS JAM-PACKED JAMBOREE

Published in the UK by Titan Books, a division of Titan Publishing Group,
144 Southwark St., London SE1 0UP, under licence from Bongo Entertainment, Inc.

FIRST EDITION: JANUARY 2005

ISBN 1-84576-228-2
2 4 6 8 10 9 7 5 3 1

Publisher: MATT GROENING
Creative Director: BILL MORRISON
Managing Editor: TERRY DELEGEANE
Director of Operations: ROBERT ZAUGH
Art Director: NATHAN KANE
Art Director Special Projects: SERBAN CRISTESCU
Production Manager: CHRISTOPHER UNGAR
Legal Guardian: SUSAN A. GRODE

Trade Paperback Concepts and Design: SERBAN CRISTESCU

Contributing Artists:
KAREN BATES, TIM BAVINGTON, JOHN COSTANZA, LEA HERNANDEZ, JASON HO, NATHAN KANE,
OSCAR GONZALEZ LOYO, BILL MORRISON, KEVIN M. NEWMAN, PHYLLIS NOVIN, PHIL ORTIZ, RICK REESE,
MIKE ROTE, HORACIO SANDOVAL, STEVE STEERE, JR., CHRIS UNGAR, ART VILLANUEVA

Contributing Writers:
IAN BOOTHBY, ABBY DENSON, CHUCK DIXON, DAN FYBEL
JESSE LEON MCCANN, GAIL SIMONE

PRINTED IN CANADA

WILDERNESS GUIDE

JUDGE
MARGE

TO THE *GALLOWS*, KIRK VAN HOUTEN! FROM THERE YOU WILL BE DRAWN AND QUARTERED...

...ANY BODY PARTS STILL *ALIVE* WILL THEN FACE THREE CONSECUTIVE *LIFE SENTENCES.*

IAN BOOTHBY
SCRIPT

OSCAR GONZALEZ LOYO
PENCILS

PHYLLIS NOVIN
INKS

ART VILLANUEVA
COLORS

KAREN BATES
LETTERS

BILL MORRISON
EDITOR

MATT GROENING
COURT REPORTER

THAT'S THE SENTENCE I *WISH* I COULD GIVE YOU DEADBEAT DADS!

BUT SINCE THIS IS A *SMALL CLAIMS TV COURT,* I FINE YOU $400.

HEH, HEH! I LOVE HOW JUDGE JULIE GOES AFTER *LOUSY FATHERS* WHO DON'T GIVE THEIR KIDS WHAT THEY *NEED.*

I STILL GET THE $500 FEE FOR APPEARING ON THE SHOW, RIGHT?

IX-NAY ON THE EE-FAY!

DAD, I NEED *GLASSES!*

HERE'S A PAIR I FOUND IN FLANDERS' TRASH!

WHAT'CHA GOT, LIS? LAZY EYE?

HARDLY. I HAVE WHAT MY OPTOMETRIST CALLS *OVERACHIEVING EYE.*

DAD, I CAN'T WEAR *SOMEONE ELSE'S* GLASSES.

LISA, WE COULD FIGHT ALL DAY ABOUT THIS, OR WE COULD ASK THE *MAGIC ANSWER BOX.*

YOU MEAN THE *TV?*

SHHHH! IT'S *TALKING.*

HI, EVERYBODY!

HI, DR. NICK!

WELCOME TO MY PHONE IN SHOW WHERE I ANSWER ALL YOUR QUESTIONS ABOUT *MEDICALNESS* AND *DOCTOROLOGY*.

UH... DR. NICK?

SORRY.

NURSE SAMSON, PLEASE! I'M TRYING TO HOST A SHOW HERE.

BEEEEEEEEEEEEEEEP!

CALLER ONE, YOU ARE ON THE AIR!

HELLO, DR. NICK, I HAVE A QUESTION ABOUT GLASSES FOR MY DAUGHTER. ARE ALL PRESCRIPTIONS THE SAME?

EXCUSE ME. NURSE, COULD YOU TURN THAT HEART MONITOR OFF? THAT *LONG SUSTAINED BEEP* IS SO *ANNOYING* TO THE *EAR HOLES!*

BEEEEEEEEEEEEEEEEEEP!

BUT BACK TO YOUR QUESTION. YES, ALL PRESCRIPTIONS ARE THE SAME. JUST LIKE DAILY WEAR THROWAWAY CONTACT LENSES WERE THE SAME AS THE REGULAR KIND.

IT'S ALL A BIG *EYE DOCTOR* SCAM.

SPEAKING OF SCAMS. FUNNY STORY. IT ALSO TURNS OUT *ALL KNOWN DISEASES* CAN BE CURED BY A SIMPLE *HOUSE-HOLD PRODUCT*.

STOP HIM! HE'LL RUIN US ALL!

THE PRODUCT IS...

NOOO!

WE *WARNED* YOU!

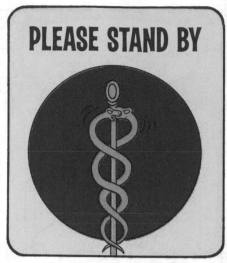

PLEASE STAND BY

SO YOU SEE LISA, THERE'S NO REASON TO BE AFRAID OF GETTING YOUR *TONSILS* OUT.

THIS IS ABOUT MY NEEDING GLASSES!

EWWW! YOU REALLY GOT THESE FROM MR. FLANDERS' TRASH?

IF BY *"TRASH"* YOU MEAN *"FROM HIS FACE WHILE HE WAS ASLEEP IN HIS HAMMOCK,"* THEN YES.

MEANWHILE...

SCREEECH!

CRASH!

DADDY, SHOULD YOU BE DRIVING WITHOUT YOUR GLASSES?

BEING *LEGALLY BLIND* IS NO EXCUSE FOR *MISSING CHURCH.* FAITH WILL GUIDE US STRAIGHT AND TRUE!

HERE WE ARE!

UM... DADDY?

NO TIME TO TALK, ROD. YOU AND TODD GO GRAB A *GOOD PEW* WHILE I FIND A PARKING SPACE.

HARI KRISHNA TEMPLE
WELCOME ALL

I GUESS I COULD AT LEAST *TRY* MR. FLANDERS' GLASSES.

AAAAAH!

IT'S LIKE MY EYES WERE SOAKED IN *SUGAR!*

WHAT'S ALL THE *YELLING?* DID NEW ZEALAND INVADE? I TRIED TO WARN THE PRESIDENT, BUT WOULD HE LISTEN?

OH, HI, GRAMPA. I'M YELLING BECAUSE I NEED GLASSES FOR ONE OF MY EYES.

SOCIAL

I MIGHT BE ABLE TO HELP.

YEP, *HERE* IT IS!

A *MONOCLE?* DID YOU GET THIS FROM A *GERMAN OFFICER?*

KINDA. I *STOLE* IT FROM WERNER KLEMPERER'S DRESSING ROOM WHEN I WAS A *SECURITY GUARD* FOR TV'S "HOGAN'S HEROES."

OH MY GOSH! I CAN SEE *PERFECTLY.* THANKS, GRAMPA.

9

AS LONG AS IT'S AFTER *SCHOOL HOURS* OR ON *WEEKENDS*, I'LL DO IT!

YAY!

HUZZAH!

HOORAY!

BOOOOOOO!

WHAT?

THE NEXT DAY...

HEY, LISA! GIMME YOUR *LUNCH MONEY!*

I WILL NOT. I NEED THAT MONEY FOR A *WELL-BALANCED MEAL!*

O-OKAY LISA! WE DON'T WANT ANY *TROUBLE!* LET'S GET OUTTA HERE!

HMMMMM.

MEANWHILE...

NOW, SOME OF YOU MAY BE ASKING WHY WE'RE IN *THE MALL FOOD COURT*. THE *REAL* COURT WAS RENTED OUT FOR *BINGO* THIS WEEK, AND WE COULDN'T AFFORD TO GIVE THE DEPOSIT BACK.

FIRST UP, SNAKE. YOU ARE ACCUSED OF *CAR THEFT*. HOW DO YOU PLEAD?

I'VE *NEVER* STOLEN A CAR IN MY LIFE, DUDE!

THEN WHY ARE YOU *MR. JUNE* IN THE NEW *CAR THIEF SWIMSUIT CALENDAR?*

MMMM...MMMM. HE'S *GRAND THEFT AUTO-EROTIC!*

THE NEXT DAY...

GET YOUR *FREE SAMPLE* OF OUR NEW ORGANIC FRUIT SNACKS!

I'D LIKE AN ORGANIC FRUIT SNACK.

TAKE THEM ALL, JUST DON'T *HURT ME!*

THIS MONOCLE SEEMS TO BRING WITH IT *RESPECT* AND *FEAR*. BUT I CAN'T LET IT *GO TO MY HEAD*.

I WANT FREE SAMPLES, AND I WANT THEM *NOW!*

YES, MA'AM!

SNAP!

WE'LL BE *BROADCASTING* YOUR NEXT FEW CASES *LIVE* ON THE NEWS, TO SEE IF YOU'RE READY TO HAVE YOUR OWN *TV SERIES*.

LIKE JUDGE JULIE?

HER SHOW'S BEEN PUT ON *HIATUS*.

"SHE WAS DETAINED IN TIJUANA FOR REASONS I'M NOT AT LIBERTY TO DISCUSS."

OKAY, OKAY. LET'S MAKE SURE WE GET OUR STORIES STRAIGHT.

YOU *STILL* WANT TO *MARRY ME*, RIGHT, KRUSTY?

I SURE DO! A WIFE CAN'T *TESTIFY* AGAINST HER HUSBAND *HERE*, TOO. *RIGHT?!!*

SERGIO ESTUVO AQUÍ!

XXX

NOW REMEMBER, PEOPLE ARE CRAZY ABOUT YOUR *UNFLAPPABLE DISCIPLINARIAN THING.*

KEEP THAT UP, AND YOU'LL BE A *STAR!*

HEAR ME, HEAR ME! COURT IS NOW IN SESSION! FIRST CASE ON THE DOCKET IS...

WHACK!

WHAT'S UP, DOCKET?

AAAAAH!

BART!

PRINCIPAL SKINNER, WHAT ARE YOU DOING IN YOUR *MOTHER'S DRESS?*

I'LL HAVE YOU KNOW THIS IS *MY* DRESS!

HA, HA!

I MEAN *MY ROBE!* I MEAN, STOP SKATEBOARDING IN MY COURT!

HE'S LOST *CONTROL* OF HIS OWN COURT!

NO ONE CAN STOP THAT *WILD CHILD!*

ALL IS LOST!

BART!

¡GULP!¿

WELL, YOU SHOULD HAVE THOUGHT OF THAT *BEFORE* ALL YOUR *CRIMINAL MASTERMINDING!*

FINE! FINE! *I CONFESS!* JUST STOP THE *SCOLDING!*

FANTASTIC WORK TODAY, MARGE! YOUR NELSON RATINGS ARE THROUGH THE ROOF!

YOU MEAN *NIELSEN* RATINGS.

NO, I MEAN NELSON.

YOU KICK BUTT!

THE NIELSEN FAMILY DIED OFF YEARS AGO DUE TO *INBREEDING*. NOW WE RELY ON SMALL CHILDREN, THE ELDERLY, AND THE OCCASIONAL ESCAPED MENTAL PATIENT FOR *RATINGS*.

SUDDENLY, TELE-VISION MAKES A LOT MORE *SENSE*.

MEANWHILE...

HEY, HOMER. YOU EVER NOTICE WHEN MOM GETS A JOB THINGS *FALL APART* HERE AT HOME?

YES. YES I HAVE. I MEAN, NORMALLY LISA HELPS OUT AS THE *VOICE OF REASON,* BUT LATELY...

I'M TAKING YOUR PIGGY BANK AND GOING SHOPPING. *ANY OBJECTIONS?*

NO, LISA.

GOOD. CARRY ON.

ANYWAY, I FELT WE COULD USE AN *AUTHORITY FIGURE,* SO THE HOUSE DOESN'T GET *CONDEMNED* AGAIN.

BUT WHO, BART? WHO?

JUDGE SNYDER! HE'S HEALTHY AGAIN, AND NOW THAT MOM'S TAKEN OVER, HE'S *OUT OF WORK.*

HOW DID I MISS HIM STANDING RIGHT THERE?

I'VE BEEN A FAMILY COURT JUDGE FOR TWENTY YEARS. *I'LL WORK FOR FOOD.*

YOU'RE *HIRED.* NOW QUIT BLOCKING THE TV, YOUR HONOR!

I'LL JUST TAKE OUT THE MONOCLE, AND...

WHAT?

NO!

NEVER TAKE IT OUT! THE MONOCLE IS *FEAR!* THE MONOCLE IS *POWER!*

BUT, DO I WANT PEOPLE *TO FEAR ME?*

DUH! LOOK AT ALL THE *STUFF* YOU GOT TODAY! AND THERE'S *MORE TO COME!*

HOW MUCH MORE?

NO! THIS IS *WRONG! THE POWER IS CORRUPTING ME!*

THIS ENDS NOW!

NOOOOOOO!

LISA, GREAT NEWS! THE WERNER KLEMPERER FAN CLUB CALLED ME. THEY'RE OFFERING $50,000 FOR THE MONOCLE.

D'OH!

LATER THAT NIGHT AT THE (FOOD) COURT...

CAN'T WE WRAP IT UP NOW? I'M *EXHAUSTED* AND I *MISS MY FAMILY.*

NO! WE *OWN* YOU, MARGE. IN FACT, WE'D LIKE YOU TO START SLEEPING IN YOUR TRAILER INSTEAD OF GOING HOME AT NIGHT.

NOW FOR THE NEXT CASE...

WHAT THE...

MARGE, HONEY, *WE NEED YOU BACK!*

4.95

$5.50

THE PLACE IS A *MESS*. I'M UNDER *HOUSE ARREST* AND CAN'T LEAVE HOME WITHOUT WEARING THIS *LEG BAND* THAT SHOCKS ME EVERY TWENTY SECONDS.

AAAAAH!

BART'S RUNNING THINGS, AND LISA'S UNDER A MONOCLE'S *EVIL POWER*.

NO, I'M NOT. I GOT OVER THAT *THIS AFTERNOON*.

WELL, THANKS FOR *KEEPING ME IN THE LOOP*. NOW I LOOK LIKE AN *IDIOT*.

AAAAAH!

OH, HOMER! I WISH I *COULD* QUIT, BUT THEY HAVE ME UNDER *CONTRACT*. THEY COULD *SUE*!

UM...MOM, YOU SIGNED THIS CONTRACT "JUDGE MARGE." IF YOU'RE NOT A JUDGE ANYMORE, IT'S *NOT VALID*.

I QUIT!

RRRIP!

WAIT! YOU CAN'T!

BUT ONE FINAL *JUDICIAL ACT*! YOU'RE HELD *IN CONTEMPT* UNTIL I'M GONE!

COME ALONG YOU!

ALL RIGHT!

WAY TO GO MARGE!

NOW, LET'S ALL GET SOME ICE CREAM!

YAY!

SO, JUDGE SNYDER'S BEING REINSTATED RIGHT NOW?

YEP, AND AS A FORMER JUDGE, I HAVE A *GET OUT OF JAIL FREE CARD.*

OH, HOW CUTE. LIKE MONOPOLY. HEY, WAIT! THIS IS *REAL.*

AAAAAH!

ARE YOU OKAY, HOMEY?

YEAH, THE *POLICE* SAID THEY'D TAKE THE LEG BAND OFF WITHIN *FIVE BUSINESS DAYS.* THE ICE CREAM STOPS THE *INTERNAL ELECTRICAL BURNS* PRETTY GOOD, THOUGH.

AAAAAH!

WELL, YOU KNOW WHAT THEY SAY. "I SCREAM, YOU SCREAM, WE ALL SCREAM FOR ICE CREAM." HEE, HEE!

C'MON, MOM. DAD'S REALLY *SUFFERING.*

YOU'RE RIGHT. I'M SORRY.

AAAAAH!

HA! HA! HA! HA! HA!

THE END

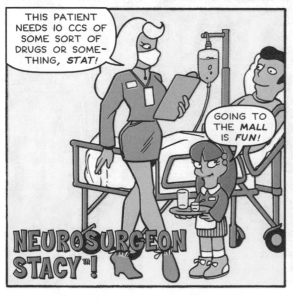

BOY, I'M *TIRED* AFTER WEARING ALL THOSE *OUTFITS!* GUESS IT'S TIME FOR *YOU* TO GET READY FOR YOUR *BIG DATE* WITH MALIBU TAD, RIGHT, STACY?

NOT YET, MUFFY! THERE'S STILL PLENTY OF TIME FOR...

...MALIBU STACY'S *FUN PAGES!*

Malibu Mail!

Send all letters to:
Malibu Mail,
c/o Petrochem
Petrochemical Corporation
Springfield, USA

Well, we've got lots of letters in our mailbag this month, so let's get right to them, shall we?

Dear Malibu Stacy,
Congratulations on another fabulous issue. I must admit, the suspense when Malibu Tad asked you if you'd go to the big dance was unbearable! Kudos to the entire crew at *Malibu Stacy Comics* for their masterful story-telling.

However, I do have one small complaint...on page one of *"Stacy's Beach Brunch Bunch,"* the dots on her fashionable two-piece swimsuit are light red--and yet, just a page later, they're dark pink. How could this be?

I'm pleasingly puzzled!

Your biggest fan,
Waylon Smithers

*Well, I must say, you certainly **ARE** a sharp-eyed little girl! However, it's easy to explain. I got a little bit of nasty ol' sand on my suit, so, of course, I had to run and change! But thanks for paying such close attention to my stories, and congratulations to your parents for giving you such an unusual and charming name!*

Dear Malibu Stacy,
I'm in fourth grade. There's this boy I like, but I'm not sure if he likes me. What should I do?

Tina Pemberton

This one's easy! Simply find out what this boy likes, and completely change your likes and personality to match his. Some of the best solutions are the simplest ones! Let me know how it turns out, Tina!

Dear Malibu Stacy,
I'm eight years old, and I go to Springfield Elementary. I love your adventures and your carefree attitude. I've drawn a picture of you, which I've included.

Lisa Simpson

P.S. If this is considered trespassing on your copyrighted image, please forgive me, as I am unaware of the legal consequences.

Dear Lisa,

I would never wear green with orange.

Well, that's all for this month! Join us next month for my next thrilling adventure, "Never Enough Shoes!"

THE WELL-DRESSED *END!*

SOON...

DUFF BEER IS *PROUD* TO ANNOUNCE THE WINNER OF OUR *CARIBBEAN ESCAPE!*

A MAN WHO *KNOWS* THE FROSTY AMBER GOODNESS OF DUFF AND DRINKS A *LOT* OF IT!

THAT'S *ME!*

YOU AND YOUR FAMILY WILL SPEND TWO WEEKS ON *SANDY BEACHES* UNDER A *TROPICAL SUN* THANKS TO *DUFF!*

WOW. *BIG* TICKETS.

TO SYMBOLIZE THE BIG *FUN* YOU'LL BE HAVING!

BOSQUEVERDE? BUT ISN'T THAT PLACE A GODAWFUL--

--FULLY *WONDERFUL* PARADISE ISLAND OF BEAUTY AND JOY?

YOU *BET,* LITTLE GIRL!

WHO *SAYS* DRINKING BEER TO WIN A CONTEST MAKES YOU A LOSER?

YOU DID, DAD.

IN YOUR *FACE!*

I HAVE JUST... **MOVED** IN. THE PLACE REALLY ISN'T "ME" YET.

THIS MUST BE THE BIGGEST HOUSE IN THE **WORLD**.

SADLY, THAT IS NOT TRUE, NIÑO.

THERE IS ANOTHER, MUCH **LARGER** HOUSE.

¿DAQUIRI, SEÑOR?

ARE YOU MARRIED, GENERAL?

AH, SÍ. MY WIFE WILL BE IN AFTER SHE IS FINISHED **SINGING** ON THE BALCONY.

♪ DON'T CRY FOR ME, BOSQUEVERDE. ♪ YOUR TEARS MEAN NOTHING TO ME. I WONDER WHYYYY EVERY NIIIGHT- ♪ YOU COME TO SEEEE ME. ♪

♪ WE HAVE NO TEE-VEEEEEE... ♪

Dear Diary,
While everyone else enjoys the hospitality of our despotic host, I choose to explore Bosqueverde's natural splendor.

This is nature undisturbed by man or mini-mall.

AH.

I'll have to look this woodland friend up in "Little Ms. Know-it-all's Book of Creatures".

RARRRRRRR!

YAAAAAAH!

?

In fact, I think I'll go get that book right away.

OH, NO!

GENETICALLY-ALTERED FOOD!

KRIS KRISTOFFERSON.

VIVA LA REVOLUCIÓN, MI AMIGA.

SHERYL CROW.

NICE TO SEE YOU.

ALEC BALDWIN.

I'VE *GOT* TO STOP SAYING I'LL LEAVE THE COUNTRY EVERY TIME SOMEONE I DON'T LIKE RUNS FOR OFFICE.

THE GUY WHO PLAYED URKEL.

WHAT CAN I *SAY*? IT'S A *GIG*.

I HATE TO *SAY* THIS, BUT EVEN FOR A GUERILLA LAIR THIS IS PRETTY LOW RENT.

TELL ME ABOUT IT. IF NOT FOR THE MONEY FROM TED TURNER, WE WOULD BE IN EVEN WORSE SHAPE.

AND EVEN *HE* MAKES DEMANDS OF US.

WHAT WE NEED ARE *FRESH* IDEAS FOR DISRUPTING GENERAL HIDALGO'S PUPPET STATE.

IDEAS THAT DO NOT REQUIRE MUCH *CASH* OUTLAY.

COMANDANTE, I MAY HAVE THE SOLUTION TO *ALL* YOUR PROBLEMS.

WATCH NCAA ACTION ON TNT

BART?

BART?

BART!

BART, IT'S *ME!*

AYE CARUMBA!

WATCH YOUR LANGUAGE IN FRONT OF MY *NIÑO!*

OW!

SLAP!

WHAT'D I SAY?

HEY, WHERE'VE YOU *BEEN*, LIS'? *MOM* WAS LOOKING FOR YOU.

NO TIME FOR THAT. LISTEN *UP*, BART. THIS MAY BE THE OPPORTUNITY OF A *LIFETIME.*

LET ME GET THIS *STRAIGHT*...

YOU WANT ME TO HELP YOU PLAY MINDLESS PRANKS AND POSSIBLY DANGEROUS PRACTICAL JOKES TO DISRUPT THE STATUS QUO OF YOUR WHOLE *COUNTRY?*

JUST THINK OF GENERAL HIDALGO AS PRINCIPAL SKINNER.

TEMPTING... TEMPTING...

REVOLUTION FOR THE *HELL* OF IT?

SIGN ME *UP!*

!GENERAL!

THE PRESIDENT OF THE UNITED STATES IS ON THE PHONE!

I'LL TAKE IT ON LINE TWO.

SEÑOR PRESIDENTE, HOW MAY I *ASSIST* YOU?

I'M LOOKING FOR ONE OF MY AMBASSADORS.

ALLOW ME TO *HELP*.

HER NAME IS *MARY COHEN*.

I SHALL *ASK* FOR HER.

POR FAVOR. HAS ANY ONE SEEN MARY COHEN?

I AM *LOOKING* FOR A MARY COHEN. WILL SOMEONE FIND A *MARY COHEN* FOR ME?

WHAT IS SO *HUMOROSO?*

:SNORT!:

MARICON... :GIGGLE:.*

*MARICON=SISSY

WHERE *IS* THIS MARY COHEN I SEEK?

HA! HA! HA! HA! HA! HA! HA! HA! HA! HA!

THE PSYCHOLOGICAL PHASE OF MY ATTACK HAS BEGUN.

NOW WE GET *SERIOUS*.

YOU SAY YOU ARE WILLING TO *TELL* ME THE IDENTITY OF THIS VANDAL WHO PLAGUES MY EVERY WAKING MOMENT?

AND WHAT DO YOU WISH IN *RETURN*...

...*SEÑOR SKINNER*?

NOT A *THING*, GENERAL, SO LONG AS YOU *KEEP* HIM IN YOUR COUNTRY UNTIL HE'S EIGHTEEN.

The Springfield Shopper

BOSQUEVERDE PLAGUED BY PRANKSTER

THIS TOMFOOLERY HAS ALL THE EARMARKS OF ONE BART SIMPSON OF SPRINGFIELD, U.S.A.

The Springfield Shopper

SO, OUR GUESTS HAVE GONE FROM TOURIST TO *TERRORIST*.

I WANT THEM TO BE *FOUND* AND TO MEET WITH AN UNFORTUNATE AND *HORRIFYING* ACCIDENT!

MOM!

MOM!

WHAT *IS* IT, KIDS?

LISA GOT ME TO JOIN SOME REBEL FRIENDS OF HERS, AND NOW THE ARMY HAS ORDERS TO SHOOT TO *KILL* ME.

IT'S *TRUE*, MOM! BART MAY HAVE ACTUALLY *OVER-ACHIEVED* THIS TIME.

WELL, I GUESS WE'LL HAVE TO GET YOUR *FATHER* AND SEE ABOUT LEAVING.

EL CASINO GRANDE

YOU WIN *AGAIN*, SEÑOR SIMPSON.

I AM *NEVER* LEAVING THIS PLACE!

LOOK AT ALL THIS *MOOLAH*!

YOU HAVE WON *EIGHTEEN MILLION* BOSQUEVERDAN *CHU-CHUS*.

HOW MUCH IS IT IN *AMERICAN*?

I SHALL *CALCULATE* IT, SEÑOR.

HOMER, WE'RE ALL IN GREAT *DANGER*!

WE GOTTA LEAVE *NOW*, DAD!

WHAT? AND LEAVE A *FORTUNE* BEHIND?

IT IS *SIX DOLLARS AND TWENTY-NINE CENTS* IN YOUR DOLLARS, SEÑOR.

SEE?

THERE THEY ARE!

ALL BETTING IS CLOSED UNTIL THE EXECUTION IS OVER.

WE HAVE TO *RUN*, DAD!

MY FAMILY IS GOING TO BE MURDERED...AND ON *FAJITAS NIGHT*!

BLAM!

BLAM!

THE NORTEAMERICANOS ARE TO BE *BUTCHERED* BY OUR OPPRESSORS!

THIS IS THE MOMENT WE HAVE *WAITED* FOR.

YES! THEY WILL MAKE A *TELEVISION* MOVIE ABOUT THIS!

BY FEBRUARY SWEEPS WE COULD BE *FREE*!

WATCH NCAA ACTION ON TNT

¡ALTO, GRINGOS!

YOU WILL STAND STILL TO BE SHOT, POR FAVOR.

WHUPPA!

WHUPPA!

EEP!

BRRRRRRRT!

IF WE GET GUNNED DOWN IN A HAIL OF HOT LEAD, YOU ARE IN *BIG* TROUBLE, BOY!

SORRY, HOMESLICE!

INTO THE *JUNGLE!* WE CAN *HIDE* THERE!

WHERE'S FLANDERS' WEED-WHACKER WHEN WE *NEED* IT?

IT'S AT HOME IN OUR *GARAGE*.

STUPID *FLANDERS!* WHAT GOOD IS IT DOING US *THERE?*

STOP RIGHT THERE!

TAKE THE *BOY! HE* DID IT!

GAAAAAAAH!

GOOD AH-FTERNOON. I AM *RAINIER WOLFCASTLE*, CURRENTLY FILMING "MCBAIN XII: THE DAY AFTER THE LAST DAY ON EARTH." WE NEED *EX*-TRAHS TO PLAY TERRIFIED AH-MERICAN HOSTAGES.

SHOW US TO OUR *TRAILER*, MR. WOLFCASTLE!

WELL, IT LOOKS LIKE WE'RE GOING HOME.

I CAN'T *WAIT*, MARGE. THIS IS THE WORST VACATION *EVER*. IT'S LIKE I'VE BEEN *CURSED!*

HEH HEH HEH HEH HEH

HEH HEH HEH HEH HEH HEH

QUIT THAT MANIACAL LAUGHTER, BARNEY.

IT'S *CREEPIN'* ME OUT.

THE END

Beauty School HELLCATS

SPRINGFIELD DEPARTMENT OF MOTOR VEHICLES...

G'ON AN' TAKE MAH PITCHER, MISSY DMV LADY! I GOTS TO GET A LICENSE IF'N I WANTS T' DRIVE MAH TRACTOR TO CHURCH ON SUNDAY!

HOLD YOUR WATER, JETHRO. YOU CAN'T RUSH ART. NOW, SMILE.

HIS LEF' SIDE GOTS A LOT MORE TEETH.

| GAIL SIMONE | JOHN COSTANZA | TIM BAVINGTON | ART VILLANUEVA/RICK REESE | KAREN BATES | MATT GROENING |
| STORY | PENCILS | INKS | COLORS | LETTERS | DRIVING INSTRUCTOR |

YA MEANS LIKE THIS?

UGH, NO.

DO YOU MIND IF I...?

WHUT TH'...?!!?

YOU GO, GAL!

JUST A LITTLE TOUCH-UP HERE AND THERE...

WHY, THESE HERE PITCHERS IS TOO *PURTY* FOR TA PUT ON A DUMB OL' LICENSE!

I...I FEELS SO UN-REPULSIVE!

LET'S GO HOME AN' COMMENCE TO SOME *BABY-MAKIN'* AFORE A BUG GETS STUCK IN YORE *BEAUTIFUL* HAIR, CLETUS!

DMV-SAT RELAY

DEE-*DEET!*

DEE-*DEET!*

DMV-1

COMMANDER! WE'RE GETTING A *DMV-SATCOM* REPORT OF A CLERK IN OUR SPRINGFIELD OFFICE--

SHE'S...SHE'S TAKING *FLATTERING LICENSE PHOTOS*, SIR!

BLAST! GET ME HER OFFICE SUPERVISOR, *NOW!*

SOON...

?

MISS BOUVIER, WOULD YOU STEP INTO MY OFFICE FOR A MOMENT PLEASE?

UH, OH.

56

SELMA, DO YOU *LIKE* WORKING HERE?

OF COURSE NOT. I *HATE* IT HERE. IT'S *DEHUMANIZING* AND *SPIRIT-CRUSHING*.

GOOD, GOOD.

I'LL BE FRANK, SELMA. UP UNTIL RECENTLY, YOU'VE NEVER SHOWN AN *OUNCE* OF CREATIVITY, NOR HAVE YOU *EVER* PERFORMED YOUR WORK WITH THE SLIGHTEST ENTHUSIASM.

IN SHORT, YOU'VE BEEN A *PERFECT EMPLOYEE*.

SO, WHY NOT TAKE A NICE, *LONG* VACATION? FIND A WAY TO *RID* YOURSELF OF THESE..."*CREATIVE IMPULSES*."

PLEASE WAIT YOUR TURN TO BE FIRED! YOU ARE NUMBER:

BECAUSE IF YOU STILL *HAVE* THEM WHEN YOU COME BACK...I'M AFRAID YOU'LL HAVE TO TAKE A *NUMBER*.

HEY, WHERE ARE *YOU* GOING?

TO ENROLL IN BEAUTY SCHOOL, LIKE I'VE ALWAYS DREAMED!

HOT DOG! HANG ON, I'M COMING WITH YOU!

OH, MAN, I *KNEW* I SHOULDN'T HAVE DRAWN THAT AWESOME HOT ROD ON MY TEST FORM!

WHAT ABOUT THE PEOPLE STILL IN LINE?

HEH. GOOD ONE. "WHAT ABOUT THE PEOPLE STILL IN LINE." HEH.

HEH. AHEH.

SOON...

PATTY, I CAN'T BELIEVE IT! I'M *FINALLY* GOING TO BEAUTY SCHOOL!

OUTDATED MAGAZINES AND UNLIMITED GOSSIP, *HERE WE COME!*

Mister Pierre's Académe of Beauty and Image (Formerly Pete's Budget Bowl Cuts)

TWO TO SIGN UP FOR CLASSES, PLEASE.

UH, WE DON'T ALLOW PETS...

I HAVE NO SENSE OF SMELL. THIS IS MY 'SMELLING-NOSE LIZARD,' JUB-JUB.

IT'S LIKE A SEEING-EYE DOG THAT DOESN'T LICK ITSELF.

WELL, OKAY...YOU'LL BE WITH THE OTHER *NEW* STUDENTS IN *MR. PIERRE'S* GROUP.

GOOD MORNING, LADIES. WELCOME TO *HAIRSTYLING HELL!*

;GULP!;

YOU *WILL* BE ISSUED ONE REGULATION *PINK SMOCK.* YOU *WILL* MASTER THE INTRICACIES OF *PRECISION HAIRCUTTING,* IF I HAVE TO *BEAT* IT INTO YOU!

THIS ISN'T "SUPERCUTS," LADIES. THIS IS *MY WORLD.*

AND TUCK IN THAT LIZARD!

DAY TWO...

WE'LL START WITH *BASIC SHAMPOOING...* THAT'S EXCELLENT WETTING TECHNIQUE, THERE, MISS PATTY.

MISS SELMA! WHAT IS YOUR *MAJOR MALFUNCTION?*

IT'S NOT MY FAULT! I CAN'T GET HIS HEAD IN THE SHAMPOO BOWL!

HELP! THIS WOMAN IS A *MENACE* TO THOSE WITH *UNUSUAL FOLLICLE ORNAMENTATION!*

DAY FOURTEEN...

MISS SELMA! THIS HAIR IS NEITHER BOUNCING *NOR* BEHAVING!

I'M *ASHAMED* TO SAY THAT ONE OF *MY* TRAINEES COMMITTED THIS *ASYMMETRICAL ATROCITY!*

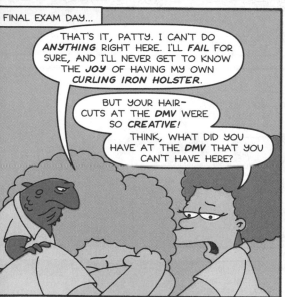

CONGRATULATIONS, SELMA. YOU'VE *EARNED* THIS DIPLOMA.

I...I NEVER WOULDA MADE IT IF NOT FOR YOU.

ARE YOU *SEEING* ANYONE CURRENTLY BY CHANCE?

≳CHOKE≳ GET THE HELL OUT OF HERE.

I'M SO PROUD OF YOU BOTH! WHAT *NEXT*? ARE YOU GOING TO *OPEN A SALON*?

NO, MY DREAM CAME TRUE ALREADY. IT'S BACK TO THE *DMV* FOR US! THEY PROBABLY HAVE A LINE OF CUSTOMERS OUT THE DOOR BY NOW.

OH YEAH. WE'D BETTER HURRY. AHEH. HEH.

HEH. AHEH, HEH!

NEXT: LIZARD MAKEOVERS!

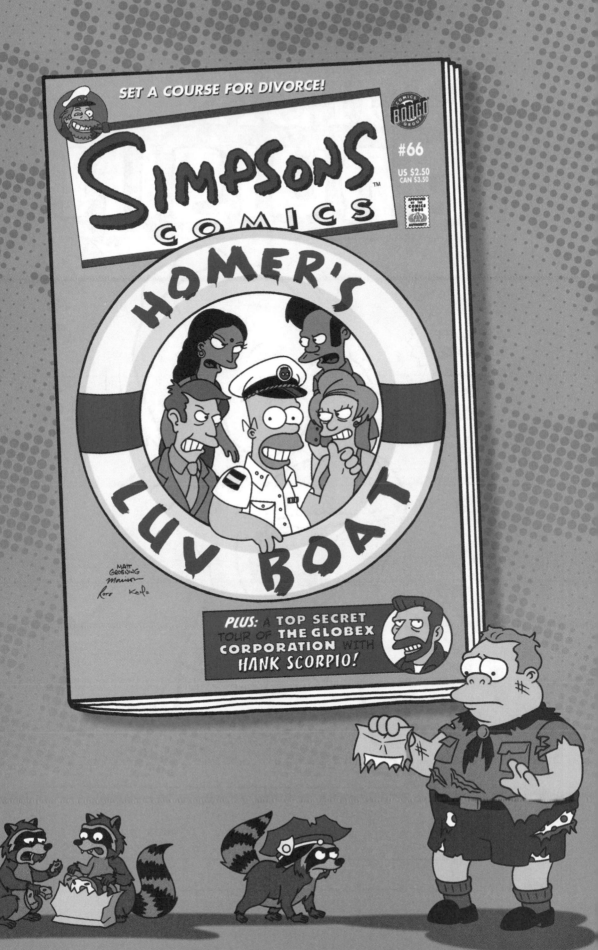

CRUISIN' for a BRUISIN'
MY WIFE IS DEAD?!!
IAN BOOTHBY SCRIPT
PHIL ORTIZ PENCILS
PHYLLIS NOVIN INKS
KAREN BATES LETTERS
ART VILLANUEVA/RICK REESE COLORS
BILL MORRISON EDITOR
MATT GROENING O CAPTAIN, MY CAPTAIN

NO, I KEEP TELLING YOU! IT'S *MY* WIFE THAT PASSED AWAY!

WHICH IS WHY I'M TRYING TO GIVE YOU OUR TICKETS TO A *ROMANTIC COUPLES CRUISE* WE BOOKED A YEAR AGO.

DID YOU SAY A *CRUISE*?

ZZIP!

WELL, I'D LIKE TO GO, FLANDERS, BUT I'M *TERRIFIED OF WATER*.

THANK YOU, NED. WE'D BE HAPPY TO TAKE YOUR TICKETS.

SWIPE!

BUT MARGE.

OH, HOMER. JUST CALL UP DR. HIBBERT AND HAVE HIM CURE YOUR *RABIES*!

AND GET RID OF THAT RACCOON!

¡SOB!¿ GOODBYE, MR. NIBBLES!

THREE DAYS AND SEVERAL PAINFUL INJECTIONS LATER...

CAPTAIN McCALLISTER'S
CRUISING ADVENTURES!
NOT ASSOCIATED WITH THE
AL PACINO FILM 'CRUISING'

WELCOME ABOARD YE' LANDLUBBIN' LOVEBIRDS!

CHECK IT OUT, MARGE! THE BARNACLES SMELL LIKE *POTPOURRI!*

NOW THAT'S CLASS!

OH, HOMER, LOOK AT THE POOL.

≅YAWN≅

OOOH, A *TRAINED DOLPHIN!*

EH!

AND IT'S *SERVING DRINKS.*

OUT OF MY WAY!

FINALLY, AN ANIMAL THAT DOES SOMETHING USEFUL BESIDES TASTE GOOD!

SO WHO ARE THESE COUPLES, HOMER?

WHAT DO YOU MEAN, BOY? YOU *KNOW* EVERYBODY.

MAYBE, I JUST LIKE HEARING EXPOSITION-STYLE CHARACTER DESCRIPTIONS, OKAY?

FINE, KNOCK YOURSELF OUT!

THERE'S PRINCIPAL SKINNER AND YOUR TEACHER MRS. KRABAPPEL. LOOKS LIKE HE'S BROUGHT HIS WORK WITH HIM, AND SHE'S NOT *TOO HAPPY* ABOUT IT.

THE NEWLY-DIVORCED LUANN VAN HOUTEN AND HER BOYFRIEND PYRO...

...AND THERE'S HER EX-HUSBAND, KIRK VAN HOUTEN, WHO'S WITH HIS *NEW GIRLFRIEND*, TENILLE.

WHERE'S SHE?

I CAN HEAR YOU, AND SHE'S RUNNING A BIT LATE, OKAY?

THERE'S APU AND MANJULA, RECENTLY BLESSED WITH *OCTUPLETS*.

HEY, HOMER, IMAGINE IF I WAS AN OCTUPLET. WOULDN'T THAT BE *COOL*?

:SHUDDER.: THAT THOUGHT IS GONNA TAKE A LOT OF BEER TO WASH AWAY.

THE MILLIONAIRE AND HIS WIFE.

THAT NIGHT...

WHERE'S YOUR *GIRLFRIEND*, MR. VAN HOUTEN?

UH...SHE'S *SEA SICK*.

WELCOME TO THE *CAPTAIN'S TABLE*. RELAX, EAT AND LET THE *LOVE VIBES* FLOW.

PASS THE PEAS?

I GUESS HE'D KNOW ABOUT *MAKING PASSES*. RIGHT, EDNA?

CAN I HAVE THE HAM THEN?

WHAT?

WHY DON'T YOU CHEW ON THIS *KNUCKLE SANDWICH*, HOMEWRECKER!

SOCK!

WHAM!

JUST IGNORE THEM! THEY'RE JUST HAVING A BOUT OF *OCEAN MADNESS*. THEY'LL GET THEIR *SEA BRAINS* SOON!

GO ABOUT YOUR *LOVE TALK!*

¿GASP!¿

MANJULA, NO! *COME BACK!*

THAT GOT THE *OLD PASSION* BACK.

PYRO! I ATE MY ENTIRE DINNER *ALONE.* YOU PROMISED YOU WOULDN'T LET YOUR *LOVE OF BATTLE* INTERFERE WITH OUR LOVE.

THIS HAS NOTHING TO DO WITH MY "AMERICAN GLADIATOR" TRAINING. I...

MAYBE WHEN YOU'RE FINISHED PLAYING WITH *YOUR FRIEND,* YOU'LL HAVE TIME FOR ME.

YOU ONLY MARRIED ME FOR *MY MONEY!*

WELL, YOU ONLY MARRIED *ME* FOR *MY* MONEY!

SO THAT'S WHY YOU WERE FIGHTING HIM? I'M SORRY FOR *SNAPPING* AT YOU. DARN THOSE *WINE SPRITZERS*. THEY TURN ME INTO A *BEAST*.

YOUR *PASSION* REMINDED ME WHY I FELL FOR YOU, LUANN VAN HOUTEN!

WELL, ALL THIS *MAKING UP* IS WELL AND GOOD FOR THE REST OF YOU, BUT WE ARE STILL NOT *MAN AND WIFE*, POSSIBLY.

AND THERE IS NOTHING ANY OF YOU CAN DO TO CHANGE THAT!

I'M CAPTAIN. YOU'RE *MARRIED*.

WELL, I CERTAINLY *SET MYSELF UP* FOR THAT!

I LOVE YOU, WIFE.

AND I YOU, HUSBAND.

AH...HAVE YOU ALL FORGOTTEN ABOUT THE PIRATES?

OH YOU'RE JUST *BITTER* BECAUSE YOUR GIRLFRIEND DOESN'T REALLY *EXIST*.

OH, YEAH. WELL, MAYBE YOUR BOYFRIEND DOESN'T EXIST, *EITHER!*

I'M RIGHT HERE.

YOU'VE WON *THIS ROUND*, LUANN!

WAIT A MINUTE! *THIS* PIRATE IS REALLY...

YANK!

CAPTAIN MCCALLISTER!

AAAR! I JUST WANTED TO RUIN YER' CRUISE LIKE *YOU* RUINED *MINE*. AND I WOULD HAVE GOTTEN AWAY WITH IT, TOO...

...IF I WERE *SMARTER*.

OH, KIRK! DID I *MISS* ANYTHING?

YOUR GIRL-FRIEND IS *REAL*?!

AND *REAL HOT*! RRRRRROWL!

YEAH! SHE'S REAL! SO *THERE*!

CAPTAIN? IS THAT YOU?

TENILLE?

WHAT THE...?

SHE'S MY DARLING WIFE I THOUGHT LOST AT SEA YEARS AGO!

WELL, I *DID* MEET HER THROUGH A LOST AT SEA *DATING SERVICE*.

SO ASIDE FROM KIRK, EVERY-ONE'S HAPPY AND IN LOVE!

I'M THE *BEST CRUISE GUY* EVER!

THE END

OH, IT'S *YOU!* AND YOU'RE *EARLY!*

LISTEN, I APPRECIATE THE EFFORT, BUT WE DON'T PAY MUCH ATTENTION TO OL' *MR. TIMECLOCK* HERE. YOU KNOW WHAT I MEAN?

WORLD'S GREATEST TYRANT

NOPE, IT'S *PEOPLE* THAT COUNT, AND JUST BY LOOKING AT YOU, I CAN TELL YOU'RE DEFINITELY *PEOPLE*.

HEY, CAN I GET YOU ANYTHING?

OH, YOU *GOTTA* TRY THESE *SOY-POPS*. THESE ARE GONNA BE *HUGE* IN THE HEALTH SNACK MARKET... THEY'RE *DELICIOUS!*

I THINK I'LL HAVE ONE MYSELF!

OKAY, I'LL BE VERY HONEST WITH YOU. THAT WASN'T DELICIOUS AT ALL. THE BOYS IN R&D CAN BUILD A *LASER DEATH-TRAP* YOU WOULDN'T BELIEVE, BUT THEY CAN'T ENGINEER A DECENT *PINEAPPLE-FLAVORED SOY-POP*, BLESS THEIR HEARTS!

GLOBE

LISTEN, I'VE GOT A GOOD FEELING ABOUT YOU. JUST LET ME ASK, FOR THE *RECORD*...

...SO YOU WANT TO WORK FOR GLOBEX, HUH?

GAIL SIMONE	OSCAR GONZALEZ LOYO	STEVE STEERE, JR.	ART VILLANUEVA	KAREN BATES	BILL MORRISON	MATT GROENING
STORY	PENCILS	INKS	COLORS	LETTERS	EDITOR	MODEL EMPLOYEE

WELL, WE *WANT* YOU TO. HONEST!

HEY, LET'S GO MEET SOME OF THE GUYS! WANT TO? OKAY, LET'S!

NOW, HERE'S A GREAT BUNCH OF GUYS. MEET *GENERAL CLAW, SCARFACE, KAHBLU KHAN,* AND *THE MONOCLE!*

HOWDY, NEW GUY!

CHARMED, I'M SURE.

I WEEL SLEET HEES THROAT!

LOOK OUT! HE'S GOING ON ANOTHER *MURDEROUS RAMPAGE!*

I WEEL *KEEL* YOU, AMERICAN *PEEG!*

HA! HO! HO! HA! HO!

KIDDING! OH, BOY, WE HAVE A LOT OF FUN AROUND HERE, DON'T WE?

OH, C'EST BON! YOU TOTALLY FELL FOR EET, MON AMI!

...AND NOW, WE KEEL HEEM FOR *TRUE!*

NO, NO, NO!

I KEEL HEEM! I MAKE OF HEEM A DINNER FOR MY *TRAINED GIANT WEASEL!*

HEY, WHY DON'T WE JUST MOVE ALONG, HUH? WHATTYA SAY, SOUND GOOD? OKAY!

I WANT TO APOLOGIZE FOR THAT. SEE, HE'S GOT THIS *TRAINED GIANT WEASEL*, AND, WELL, HE'S ALWAYS TRYING TO SHOW IT *OFF*, YOU KNOW?

EXIT

IT'S KINDA *CUTE* WHEN YOU THINK ABOUT IT, HUH?

HEY, HEY! WHOA! WHERE YA GOIN'?

EXIT

Dr. Nick Riviera IN
CRIME FAMILY PRACTICE

HI, EVERYBODY!

HI, DR. NICK!

DAN FYBEL	OSCAR GONZALEZ LOYO	MIKE ROTE	CHRIS UNGAR	KAREN BATES	MATT GROENING
STORY	PENCILS	INKS	COLORS	LETTERS	DOC HOLLYWOOD

THANKS FOR FILLING IN ON SUCH *SHORT NOTICE*. WAIT A MINUTE, AREN'T YOU THE GUY THAT WAS JUST IN THE BATHROOM STEALING TOILET PAPER?

WHAT DO YOU SAY WE TAKE SOME CALLS? LINE ONE, YOU'RE ON WITH *DR. NICK* AND SOME *STRANGE COMEDIAN!*

HELLO? I HAVEN'T *BURPED* IN FIVE HOURS. AM I *DYING*?

YES, YOU ARE. WHY NOT COME TO MY CLINIC FOR A *LOOKSEE*? HOW'S *TUESDAY* AT *NOON*?

BRAAP! I'LL BE THERE!

MY INCREDIBLY HIGH FEE WILL MAKE HIM FORGET HIS CERTAIN DEATH. DID I JUST SAY THAT *ON THE AIR*?

YOU EVER *BURP* AND *SNEEZE* AT THE *SAME TIME*? NOW, WOULD THAT BE A "*SNURP*" OR A "*BNEEZE*"? THE FUNNY THING ABOUT SNEEZING IS--

LINE TWO, I AM HERE TO MAKE YOU HEALTHY!

AN HOUR LATER...

WHAT A WONDERFUL FEELING TO HELP PEOPLE. OKAY, SEE YOU AGAIN WHEN MY *APPOINTMENT BOOK* LOOKS SKINNY!

THAT REMINDS ME OF THE TIME MY BUDDY, EARL, THE ONE WITH THE TURTLES--

GOODBYE, MR. RADIO MAN!

NOW WHERE DID I PARK MY *WHEEL THINGY*?

OH, *HERE* SHE IS!

NAB!

HELLO, DR. NICK.

ULP...HELLO, EVERYBODY.

I'LL CUT TO THE CANNOLI. YOU NEED *NEW PATIENTS* AND MY "FAMILY" NEEDS A *NEW DOCTOR*.

YOU'RE IN LUCK. I CAN MAYBE SQUEEZE YOU IN, SAY...FEBRUARY?

OR PERHAPS, SAY...*RIGHT NOW*?!

SOON...

I GOT YOUR CUSTOMERS RIGHT HERE, PALLY!

DR. NICK

BRIBERY ILLUSTRAT

EXTORTION DIGEST

WOULD YOU MIND KINDLY REMOVING THESE *SHOES* FOR ME? THEY'RE NOT MY SIZE, AND FRANKLY, I'M NOT SO FOND OF *THE STYLE*.

NURSE, MY *JACKHAMMER*! *NEXT*!

I WAS HOLDING A DOOR OPEN FOR A DEAR OLD LADY. IT WAS AN ESPECIALLY *HEAVY* DOOR.

LATER...

BOY, OH BOY. I *NEVER* WORK *THIS* MANY MINUTES IN A ROW. TIME FOR A NAP.

DR. NICK. PERHAPS YOU COULD BE OF ASSISTANCE.

HOLY HEMOGLOBIN, WHAT HAPPENED TO *YOU*?

OH THIS? YOU KNOW HOW *PLAYFUL* POLICE DOGS CAN GET SOMETIMES.

GRRR

GRRR

K-9

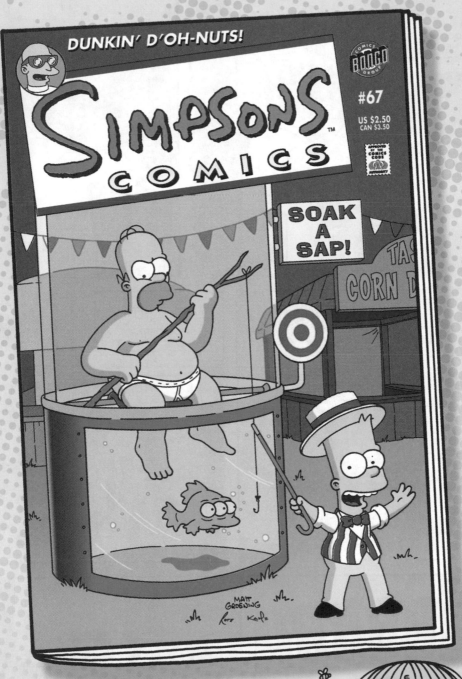

NOW, BART, I HAVE IN MY POCKET FOUR SHINY QUARTERS. YOU CAN GO AND BUY *SEVERAL* NEW COMICS, AND MAYHAP A *FESTIVE PENNYWHISTLE*, AND STILL HAVE TUPPENCE REMAINING!

THAT COMIC COST *$7.50*, HOMER.

D'OH!!

LISA! BART! I THINK I HAVE A WAY TO SOLVE *BOTH* YOUR PROBLEMS, EVEN THOUGH I'VE ALREADY FORGOTTEN WHAT LISA'S PROBLEM IS! TO THE *BASEMENT*, BOY!

WHEN *I* WAS A BOY, COMICS WERE MADE OF *FIBER-GLASS*, AND YOU HAD TO WEAR *SPECIAL GLOVES* TO READ 'EM! "*SCRATCHY DREADFULS*," WE CALLED THEM.

SEE, BOY, YOUR OLD MAN'S A *THINKER*! NOT ONLY DID I *SAVE* THE VERY *FIRST* COMIC I EVER BOUGHT, BUT I EVEN *STORED* IT IN A PLASTIC BAG TO KEEP IT IN *MINT CONDITION*!

GUESS I SHOULDN'T HAVE USED A SANDWICH BAG. *ENJOY*, SON!

BUT, *DAD...!*

THE Z-MEN

Z MEN

NOW, DON'T GO ALL *MILHOUSE* ON ME, BOY. THE LOOK IN YOUR EYES IS THANKS ENOUGH.

RASSA FRASSA STINKIN' DUMB OL' PIECE O' JUNK FUNNYBOOK, ANYWAY!

WELL, THAT'S ONE FAMILY CRISIS AVERTED IN MY OWN COMICAL STYLE. AND NOW, IT'S FINALLY *HOMER-TIME*. WHERE'S THAT REMOTE?

ONE WEEK LATER...

SURELY THERE'S SOME *WACKY, MADCAP SCHEME* TO MAKE MONEY THAT WE HAVEN'T TRIED YET...

OH, WHO AM I KIDDING? I CAN'T EVEN GET PEOPLE TO CARE ABOUT SPRINGFIELD, OUR OWN HOMETOWN. I MIGHT AS WELL GIVE UP AND CALL THE OTHERS. ⸮SIGH!⸮

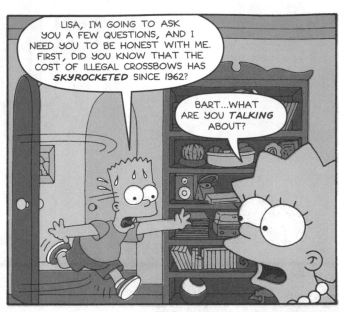

LISA, I'M GOING TO ASK YOU A FEW QUESTIONS, AND I NEED YOU TO BE HONEST WITH ME. FIRST, DID YOU KNOW THAT THE COST OF ILLEGAL CROSSBOWS HAS *SKYROCKETED* SINCE 1962?

BART...WHAT ARE YOU *TALKING* ABOUT?

NEVER MIND. DID YOU KNOW THAT DAD'S *CREDIT CARD* CHARGES **32%** INTEREST?

32%?!? ISN'T THAT *USURY*?

YOU'RE NOT HELPING, LIS...ONE MORE QUESTION...

BART, I DON'T LIKE THE SOUND OF THIS...

DO YOU KNOW ANY- ONE WHO NEEDS **10,000** PACKS OF SEEDS?

MROOWWR! HISSS!

BART, YOU'VE GOT TO MAKE THE SEED COMPANY TAKE THEM ALL BACK!

I TRIED THAT! THEY JUST *LAUGHED* AT ME!

I'M SO DEAD. TRY TO GET THEM TO SCATTER MY ASHES IN APU'S SQUISHEE MACHINE.

I'VE *GOT* IT! WE'LL GET THE ENVIRO-BEARS TOGETHER, AND WE'LL SELL THEM! IT'LL BEAUTIFY THE TOWN, AND WHAT MONEY IS LEFT AFTER PAYING OFF DAD'S CREDIT CARD WILL GO INTO THE CLUB FUND!

SCAT! SCAT!

¡AIEE! ¡PERO NÉCTAR ES *BUENO*!

BART, GET ME MY *LUCKY CLIPBOARD*.

⸮GASP!⸮

103

SOON...

ER, UH, I'M SORRY, LITTLE GIRL, BUT I'M AFRAID I'M *TOO BUSY* POLLING MY CONSTITUENTS TO BUY YOUR, UH, COOKIES, OR WHATEVER...

TEE HEE!

MISS CONGENIALITY

SAMPLES

WE NOW TAKE YOU *LIVE* TO THE DOOR OF OFF-DUTY ANCHORMAN *KENT BROCKMAN*, WHERE HIS HEARTLESS REFUSAL TO PURCHASE SEEDS IS AS WE SPEAK CRUSHING THE *ENTREPRENEURIAL SPIRIT* OF THIS BRIGHT YOUNG MAN.

JEEZ, YOU COULD JUST SAY *NO*!

SAMPLES

SORRY, LI'L LISA, BUT I'M AFRAID I CAN'T BEAUTIFY MY GARDEN ANY MORE...I'M WALKING A *FINE LINE* BETWEEN GOOD CITIZENSHIP AND PRIDEFUL-NESS AS IT IS!

SAMPLES

DEFINE IRONY: A PRECOCIOUS TOT ATTEMPTING TO PROFIT OFF OF *ME*, INSTEAD OF T'OTHER WAY 'ROUND.

DOES THAT MEAN YOU'LL BUY SEEDS?

NO! FREAKIN' *KIDS!*

MAY THE FORCE BE WITH

AMPLES

DOES YA HAVE ANY SKUNKY-CABBAGE, BLACK-EYED KUDZU, OR MAMA'S TEAT-MILKWEED?

UH, NO. WE HAVE BEGONIAS, THOUGH!

I CAIN'T FEED NO *BEGONIAS* TO MY FAMILY. THAT'S *DISGUSTIN'!*

WHOA, MAN! YOU HAVE *SEEDS*? WHERE WERE YOU FIFTEEN MINUTES AGO?

AMPLES

30-40-41-42...THAT'S IT, GANG. EIGHT DOLLARS AND FORTY-TWO CENTS IS ALL WE COLLECTED.

DON'T FORGET THAT *FIVE* OF THOSE DOLLARS CAME FROM AUNT PATTY IN RETURN FOR ME WEARING THIS *STUPID SAILOR SUIT* ALL DAY!

MY PRIDE AND TOES HURT.

WELL, I COLLECTED OVER *FORTY DOLLARS* IN THE SCHOOL CAFETERIA ALONE!

KEARNEY! THAT'S *WONDERFUL!* HOW DID YOU EVER...?

HEY, I CAN'T HELP IT IF SOME OF THE SMALLER AND MORE-EASILY-INTIMIDATED KIDS WANTED TO CONTRIBUTE THEIR LUNCH MONEY!

WELL, EVEN WITH ALL THOSE KIDS GOING HUNGRY, WE STILL AREN'T ANYWHERE NEAR OUR GOAL...

I'LL GET IT! IT MIGHT BE A LOST PIZZA DELIVERY BOY OR A DANGEROUSLY OVERLOADED GYRO TRUCK!

KNOCK! KNOCK!

KRACKA-BOOOM!!!

¡GASP!¡

AH, HELLO, CHILDREN. SELLING...*SEEDS*, I SEE. WELL, I'VE COME TO ASK YOU TO STOP IT. NO, I'VE COME TO DEMAND THAT YOU CEASE YOUR SEED-SELLING THIS INSTANT!

STOP SELLING SEEDS? BUT WHY, MR. BURNS?

LET ME MAKE THIS VERY CLEAR, CHILDREN. I AM *ALLERGIC* TO GROWING THINGS. DO YOU THINK I BUILT THE MOST TOXIC *NUCLEAR PLANT* IN THE COUNTRY ON ACCIDENT? *PISH TOSH!*

SO YOU WILL DESIST YOUR PETTY *SEED-SELLING TOM-FOOLERY* AT *ONCE!* FOR IF YOU DO NOT...

...I WILL TAKE *DRASTIC* MEASURES! YOU HAVE BEEN *WARNED.*

THE NEXT DAY...

HEY, GUYS! CAN I COUNT ON YOU BOTH TO COME TO THE BIG TOWN FAIR TONIGHT?

MR. BURNS AIN'T GONNA BE TOO *HAPPY* WITH ANY OF HIS WORKERS GOIN' TO YOUR *FAIR* THERE, HOMER.

UMM...

WHAT? WHY DO YOU SAY THAT?

WELL, MAINLY ON ACCOUNTA THIS SIGNED DOCUMENT.

Notice of Intimidation

To all Plant Employees,

Regarding the so-called "Town Fair":
Anyone caught attending this repulsive tractor pull/hog-calling contest shall be soundly beaten and then dismissed, or otherwise harassed by thugs, and not those nice thugs shown in many delightful gangster comedies, either. That is all.

Sincerely,

C. Montgomery Burns

OH, SO YOU GUYS CAN'T DO ANYTHING WITH- OUT MR. BURNS' *APPROVAL* NOW, IS THAT IT? WHAT IS HE, YOUR *MOMMY* OR SOMETHING?

HEY, THAT'S NOT *FAIR!* YOU WORK FOR MR. BURNS, *TOO,* YOU KNOW!

WHAT'S THE MATTER, LENNY? CAN'T TAKE THE *HEAT* WHEN *MOMMY MCBURNS* ISN'T AROUND?

YEP. YOUR MOMMY IS A *WITHERED OLD MAN.* IN YOUR *FACE,* CARL!

QUIT SAYING THAT, HOMER. IT'S DISTURBING!

HOMER SIMPSON SEEMS TO BE AGITATING YOUR WORKER BEES IN *SECTOR 7-G,* SIR.

REALLY? WELL, NOTHING OILS THE *MACHINERY OF CAPI- TALISM* LIKE *SPIRITED DEBATE,* YOU KNOW! BEST OF LUCK TO THAT *RABBLE-ROUSING BEATNIK!*

SHALL I HAVE HIM *BEATEN,* SIR?

OH, YES. *THRICE,* I'D SAY!

GOD *BLESS* THE FALL OF THE *SOVIET SECRET POLICE.* THESE BRIGHT YOUNG CHAPS COST ABOUT A *THIRD* OF WHAT *MAFIA* KNEE- BREAKERS NORMALLY CHARGE!

FFFSSSHHH!

CLICK!

SMITHERS! WHERE ARE THOSE GAY LIGHTS AND MERRY SOUNDS COMING FROM? THE TOWN SQUARE? SURELY THEY'RE NOT HAVING THEIR CURSED "FAIR" AGAINST MY WISHES?

AH...IT APPEARS SO, MR. BURNS!

HEY, MOE! HOW'S *BUSINESS*?

UH, NOT TOO GOOD THERE, LISA. EVEN WITH THE *FREE SEEDS* I AIN'T SEEIN' NO *ACTION*. I CAN'T FIGURE IT NO HOW!

Kissing Booth

Come and get him, ladies! Only 2 dollars!

KRAZY KAJUN SEED-FILLED FRITTERS

OH, GOOD LORD!

OH, RIGHT! THE *FACE*! I FORGOT MY UGLY *FACE* AN' ALL! NOW DON'T THAT BEAT EVERYTHING?

AAIIIEEE!

AND HEY, AIN'T YOU SUPPOSED TO BE OVER AT THE *GAZEBO*? THEY BEEN LOOKIN' *ALL OVER* FOR YOU...SCOOT ALONG NOW OR THE FLAG WILL BE *ROOINED*!

BUT I HAVEN'T SEEN THE FAIR YET!

HEAR YE, HEAR YE! COME *ONE* AND *ALL*! COME AND WITNESS THE ETERNAL STRUGGLE OF *MAN* AND *NATURE* IN A GRIM TABLEAU OF SURVIVAL AGAINST THE ODDS!

AYE, BOSUN! I'LL MEET YER SALTY CHALLENGE! 'TIS A GOODLY *CLOWN-DUNKIN'* I FORSEE!

HEY, HEY! LOOK EVERY-ONE! *POPEYE* HERE THINKS HE'S GOING TO PUT THE *CLOWN* IN THE *WATER*! GIVE ME YOUR BEST *SHOT*, AHAB!

WHIFF!

MISS!

DUNK A CLOWN! AND GET FREE SEEDS! FREE BALLS-45!

120

121

CAN'T YOU, I DON'T KNOW...*ARREST* HIM OR SOMETHING? HE'S BECOMING A *NUISANCE!*

WHAT, ARREST OL' DOC COLOSSUS? AWW...

"...YOU DON'T REALLY WANT ME TO ARREST THE POOR GUY, DO YA? I MEAN, LET'S FACE IT..."

"...HE'S *COMPLETELY* HARMLESS."

:SNIFF!:

THANKS FOR THE RIDE, EDDIE.

HEY, CHIN UP, DOC! I'M SURE YOU'LL BE BACK TA COMMITIN' MAJOR CRIMES WIT' DEM BOOTS O' YOURS ANY DAY NOW! YOU TAKE HER EASY, ALL RIGHT?

BAH.

THAT'S THE SPIRIT!

YOU HAVE *ONE* MESSAGE.

HELLO, DR. COLOSSUS? THIS IS *GENERAL KLAW* FROM THE *SECRET SOCIETY OF EVIL GENIUSES.* I'M AFRAID WE'VE VOTED TO *REVOKE* YOUR *MEMBERSHIP.* YOU'RE JUST TOO *EMBARRASSING.* CALL ME, WE'LL PLAY *BRIDGE* SOMETIME.

:SIGH.:

IT'S TRUE. IT'S *ALL TRUE.* COLOSSUS *IS* A FAILURE AS A CRIMINAL MASTERMIND!

ALL I WANT IS TO CAUSE PEOPLE TO *FLEE IN TERROR*...IS *THAT* TOO MUCH TO ASK?

FLAP!
FLAP!
FLAP!
FLAP!

AACCK! :SPUTTER!: GAH! FILTHY CREATURES!

ONE WEEK LATER...

UH...IQ OF 203, ADVANCED DEGREES IN *CHEMISTRY* AND *PHYSICS*...

I JUST WANT THE JOB WITH THE *LEAST* RESPONSIBILITY.

I'M AFRAID YOU'RE JUST *TOO* OVER-QUALIFIED, MR. COLOSSUS, SIR! EVEN THE *HEAD FRY COOK* ONLY HAS A *BASIC MEDICAL DEGREE!*

ALL RIGHT, BURGER-JOCKEYS! THIS IS *TOTALLY* A *STICK-UP!*

TAP!

BAH! AMATEUR!

DUDE! I'M, LIKE, HEADIN' FOR A *HEMORRHAGE!*

SPROING!

CRASH!

SOON...

...DOCTOR COLOSSUS, A SELFLESS HERO, HAS SAVED AN *ENTIRE RESTAURANT* FROM A BLOOD-THIRSTY CRIMINAL!

IT WAS AN *ACCIDENT!* COLOSSUS IS *EVIL!* HAS THE WORLD GONE *MAD?!?*

AND THERE HE GOES, FOLKS. THE MOST *HUMBLE,* THE MOST *HEROIC* MAN I'VE EVER KNOWN.

WE LOVE YOU COLOSSUS OH, YES WE DO, WE DON'T LOVE ANYONE, AS MUCH AS YOU!

CURSE YOUR FOOLISH LOVE FOR COLOSSUS! I DESPISE YOU ALL!!!

DR. COLOSSUS
SPRINGFIELD'S GREATEST HERO!

HE WAS THE *BEST EMPLOYEE* WE *ALMOST* EVER HAD!

≥SNIFF!≤

AIL SIMONE
STORY

JOHN COSTANZA
PENCILS

PHYLLIS NOVIN
INKS

RICK REESE
COLORS

KAREN BATES
LETTERS

COLOSSO-BOOTS SUPPLIED BY
MATT GROENING

MERCHANTS OF VENGEANCE!
FREEZE PUNK! YOU'RE *BUSTED!*
POSTERS
LEFT
LORD
LOVE
A
GULP!
IAN BOOTHBY STORY
PHIL ORTIZ PENCILS
PHYLLIS NOVIN INKS
ART VILLANUEVA COLORS
KAREN BATES LETTERS
MATT GROENING HERO AT LARGE

I SAW YOU *SHOPLIFT* THAT *WATCH!*

YEAH, WELL I SAW *YOU* SHOPLIFT THREE COFFEE MUGS, A ROLODEX, AND FIVE HAIR SCRUNCHIES.

PLEASE! YOU CAN'T TURN OL' GIL IN! I *NEED* THIS SECURITY JOB! I HAVE *COCKFIGHTING GAMBLING DEBTS!*

WELL, I'LL LET YOU OFF WITH A *WARNING* THIS TIME!

GOSH, THANKS MISTER! YOU WON'T REGRET IT!

HI-DIDDILY-HO, GIL! ANY LUCK *NABBING* THOSE PESKY SHOPLIFTERS TODAY?

NONE, MR. FLANDERS, SIR.

WELL, GOSH-DIDDILY-DARN IT! THOSE *FIFTH COMMANDMENT BREAKERS* ARE BLEEDING ME *DRIER* THAN A *COMMUNION WAFER!*

MEANWHILE...

I DO NOT UNDERSTAND IT. THE *SQUISHEE SUPPLY* IS *EMPTY* AGAIN, YET WE HAVE NOT SOLD *ONE DELICIOUS CUP* ALL DAY!

MÄLK

MÄLK

MÄLK

D-DUDE! THE RUBBER PANTS WERE A G-G-GREAT IDEA!

Y-YEAH. AND I HARDLY THINK ABOUT G-G-GIRLS AT ALL ANYMORE!

ELSEWHERE...

GOT A SHIPMENT OF RADIOACTIVE MAN'S HERE!

UH...*I'LL* SIGN FOR THOSE!

THE HAPPY LITTLE ELVES

HEH, HEH!

WAIT! WAIT! CURSE MY NEED TO VISIT THE *"DANGER ROOM"* EVERY TEN MINUTES!

I BLAME *YOU*, EXTRA LARGE MOUNTAIN DEW!

YEAH, I HEAR YA! SHOPLIFTING IS A *TERRIBLE THING*, BUT I'M AFRAID I'M *HELPLESS* TO DO ANYTHING!

HEY, LOU! THE CHIEF'S *FALLEN ON HIS BACK* AGAIN!

HE'S SO *CUTE* WHEN HE DOES THAT!

HEY, GUYS! LITTLE HELP?

LATER...

A *BAG* OF PORK RINDS, APU, MY GOOD MAN!

HERE YOU ARE, MR. HOMER, SIR!

THAT WILL BE *$400*

I TAKE IT BY THE TEX AVERY-STYLE UNHINGING OF YOUR JAW THAT YOU ARE *SURPRISED* BY *OUR NEW PRICES.*

I AM AFRAID SHOP-LIFTING HAS CAUSED ME TO GO FROM *SIMPLE GOUGING* TO A *SUPER ULTRA-GOUGE.*

SOON, THE CLERK CRUSADERS PUT THEIR PLAN INTO ACTION, WITH CUTTING EDGE GADGETRY!

MAN, APU'S NEVER AROUND. THIS IS *TOO EASY*, MAN.

CLICK!

CHUTN

WHAT'S UP WITH THE NOZZLE?

YAAAA!

FWOOOOOSH!

I MUST SAY, YOUNG DOLPH, FOR ONE ABOUT TO BE ARRESTED FOR SHOP-LIFTING YOU CERTAINLY KNOW HOW TO *KEEP YOUR COOL*.

"KEEP YOUR COOL." HEH, HEH. I MUST SUBMIT THAT TO THE *KWIK-E-MART NEWSLETTER*'S "HUMOR AT WORK" SECTION.

AND SO *THE BETTER BUSINESS BATTALION* CONTINUED THEIR SHOPLIFTING CRUSADE. SUCCESS DOGPILED ON TOP OF SUCCESS.

HOLY MOSES!

AT THE TRY 'N' SAVE...

SPROING!

Inspirational Listening

SHE WANTED TO STEAL AN ALBUM, BUT I THINK WE'VE MADE THAT MINISTER'S DAUGHTER *C.D. LIGHT!*

AT A HOT DOG STAND...

LIKE, *WHAAAA!*

YOU WANTED A *WIENER*, BUT NOW YOU ARE A *LOSER*, SIR!

CLICK!

AND WITH THE DROP IN CRIME CAME BETTER PRICES FOR CONSUMERS.

BEER NOW SOLD FOR A QUARTER A GLASS!

LEADING HOMER TO GET SO DRUNK ONE NIGHT, HE AWOKE TO FIND...

THE NEXT DAY...

WELCOME TO THE *TRYOUTS* FOR *NEW B.B.B. MEMBERS*. WE WILL CONDUCT THE TRIALS USING THE *LEGION OF SUPER-HEROES'* METHOD.

PRESENT WHAT YOU HAVE TO OFFER TO THE TEAM AND WE SHALL JUDGE YOU.

CAN WE TALK FOR ONE DIDDILY OF A SECOND?

LATER.

APU — YES / NO
YES / NO
NED — YES / NO

AAR! I'D BE *HONORED* TO JOIN YER CREW!

DIDN'T YOU *APPEAR* ON A BOX OF *POISONED FISH STICKS?*

AH, THERE'S A FUNNY STORY BEHIND THAT SENSELESS TRAGEDY!

NEXT!

WE DON'T WEAR COSTUMES.

OH THIS LITTLE NUMBER IS FOR A PARTY LATER. IT'S THE *ACTUAL SUIT* WORN BY *THE PUZZLER* IN THE 1960'S *RADIOACTIVE MAN TV SERIES*. ISN'T *IT THE LIVING END?*

SILVER AGE

SORRY, YOU'RE *TOO CAMP!*

NEXT!

I...

NEXT!

NOT *ONE* MET OUR *HIGH STANDARDS OF EXCELLENCE*. OH, WELL, WHAT SHALL WE DO TONIGHT *FELLOW CRIME FIGHTERS?*

YOU TELL HIM, MR. NED. WE AGREED YOU WOULD TELL HIM.

RARE COMICS

TELL ME WHAT? HEROES DON'T KEEP *SECRETS* FROM EACH OTHER.

APU

NED

IT'S JUST THAT THERE'S NO MORE CRIME. DAVID DIDN'T STICK AROUND AFTER HE BEAT GOLIATH.

WE'RE *NOT NEEDED* ANY-MORE.

THE NEXT WEEK...

THIS YOUNG SHOPLIFTER MUST HAVE THOUGHT IT WAS SAFE TO RETURN TO A LIFE OF CRIME!

BUT THAT WAS BEFORE HE MET *THE B.B.B. BUMPER STICKER BLASTER!*

THAT'S SOME NICE APPREHENDING, MR. G!

I JUST GOT THE GOOD WORD! YOU'VE CAUGHT *FIVE* SHOPLIFTERS IN JUST ONE WEEK.

I SUPPOSE WE WERE *TOO HASTY* IN BREAKING UP OUR GROUP.

THEN WE'RE BACK?

AS LONG AS SHOPLIFTERS THREATEN OUR COMMUNITY, WE'LL BE THERE.

HUZZAH!

UH, HUH! WELL, IF *I* WERE YOU, I'D JUST TELL AUSTRALIA TO EAT MY SHORTS.

BART! LISA! THE *SCHOOL BUS* IS HERE!

GOTTA GO, HOMER!

MAN, THE BUS SURE IS *EMPTY* TODAY.

EVERYONE'S BEEN *ARRESTED* FOR SHOPLIFTING. IT DOESN'T MAKE SENSE.

DOLPH, NELSON, KEARNEY I CAN SEE...

...BUT MILHOUSE? MARTIN? SHERRI AND TERRI?

WELL, TERRI I CAN SEE. *SHE'S* THE *EVIL TWIN*, RIGHT?

SOMETHING'S GOING ON, BART.

AW, YOU'RE JUST BEING *PARANOID*.

I HOPE SO.

LATER...

AH, NOTHING LIKE AN *AFTER SCHOOL* SQUISHEE TO WASH AWAY THE *BITTER TASTE OF LEARNING*.

NEW KRUSTY KARAMEL KRUNCH? *THIS* I GOTTA TRY.

BUY!

ALERT!

ALERT!

WHAT THE...?

GAAAH!

BANG!

CRUNCH!

OH, LITTLE BART SIMPSON. WHAT *SHAME* HAVE YOU BROUGHT ON YOUR FAMILY THIS DAY?

I DIDN'T DO IT...

YES, YES, WE *ALL* KNOW YOUR *CATCHPHRASE*, SHOPLIFTER.

SHOPLIFTER? I DIDN'T STEAL ANYTHING!

LET US ALLOW THE *SECURITY TAPE* TO END THIS DEBATE.

OH, NO!

OH, *YES!* NOW PLEASE WAIT HERE WHILE I CALL THE POLICE.

LOOK! IT'S *VISHNU!*

¡GASP!¿ HE HAS *ESCAPED!* I AM SO *ANNOYED* I AM TEMPTED TO NOT EVEN SAY...

...THANK YOU. COME AGAIN!

LIS', YOU GOTTA *HELP* ME!

BART? WHAT IS IT?

142

RUN!!!

LEAP!

TO THE B.B.B.MOBILE!

WE'RE ALREADY IN IT!

THEN *ATOMIC BATTERY TO POWER* AND *TURBINES TO SPEED,* APU!

JUST DRIVE THE RV.

WHY DID YOU NOT SAY SO IN THE FIRST PLACE?

VROOOM! VROOOM!

WHERE DID THEY GO?

AUSTRALIA DECLARES WAR ON NEW ZEALAND

¡HUFF!¡ ¡PUFF!¡

¡GASP!¡

LISA, I DON'T WANT TO GET YOU IN TROUBLE, TOO. I'M GONNA TURN MYSELF IN.

OKAY!

OKAY? YOU'D LET ME TURN MYSELF IN? DON'T YOU KNOW A *BLUFF* WHEN YOU HEAR ONE? NOW HELP ME!

OKAY, OKAY! LET'S GO BACK TO *THE SCENE OF THE CRIME* AND LOOK FOR CLUES.

HE'S AS GUILTY AS GREEDO!

LOOK CLOSER. THIS HAPPENED AFTER SCHOOL AROUND SUNSET. THERE'S THE SHADOW OF THE POTATO CHIP STAND.

WHERE'S *BART'S SHADOW*?

HE'S A *GHOST!*

¡GASP!¿

NOT A GHOST, BUT A *COMPUTER-GENERATED IMAGE* USED TO *FRAME* MY BROTHER!

THERE'S *NO PROOF* I DID IT!

LOOK IN THE LOWER LEFT CORNER OF THE SCREEN.

"BART SIMPSON FRAMING® B.B.B. VISIT OUR WEBSITE AT WWW.FRAMINGBART.ORG"

OKAY, OKAY I *CONFESS!*

YOU TOLD ME TO LIVE MY LIFE, BUT THIS GROUP *WAS* MY LIFE.

FOR THE *FIRST TIME EVER* I FELT *ACCEPTED*, EVEN, DARE I SAY IT... *LOVED*.

I WANTED TO BE A MARTIAN MANHUNTER, BUT I ENDED UP A HAL JORDAN.

I ONLY HOPE YOU CAN *FORGIVE* ME.

AW, HECK! *I'D FORGIVE* YOU EVEN IF THE BIBLE DIDN'T FORCE ME TO.

YOUR KARMA IS CLEAR WITH ME AS WELL.

WELL *I'M* STILL MAD!

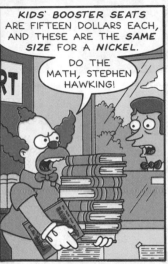

AND IF THAT WASN'T BAD ENOUGH, THE **COLLECTION PLATE** IS BARER THAN J. LO'S MIDRIFF.

NED, YOU **ALONE** TITHE MORE THAN THIS!

SORRY, REVEREND. I INVESTED ALL MY SAVINGS IN **EVANGELICAL DOT COM STOCK.**

WE NEED **MONEY** PEOPLE! THIS PLACE NEEDS A LOT OF WORK!

REMEMBER WHEN BART SIMPSON SMASHED OUR STAINED GLASS WINDOWS OF THE APOSTLES AND WE CUT CORNERS BY HIRING LENNY TO REPLACE THEM? HE DID A FINE JOB BUT...

...THE CAST OF **"THE DREW CAREY** SHOW" WAS NOT WHAT I HAD IN MIND!

MAYBE IT'S **MY** FAULT THAT WE'VE LET THINGS GO AROUND HERE.

THREE HELLFIRE SERMONS ON TITHING PER MONTH MAY BE TOO MANY. PERHAPS A LITTLE MORE TIME SPENT ON THE FUNDAMENTALS WILL PRY OPEN YOUR POCKETBOOKS.

TELL YOU WHAT. I'M GOING TO OPEN THIS SERVICE UP TO ANY **QUESTIONS** YOU HAVE ABOUT THE **MYSTERIES OF OUR FAITH.**

I'VE GOT ONE! IF YOU DRINK HOLY WATER AND TAKE A WHIZ ON A VAMPIRE, WILL YOU KILL HIM?

WHAT NAME DOES GOD SCREAM WHEN HE STUBS *HIS* TOE?

WHY ARE THE PEARLY GATES ALWAYS *GOLD* IN CARTOONS WHEN PEARLS ARE OBVIOUSLY WHITE?

WHAT DOES THE H. IN "JESUS H. CHRIST" STAND FOR?

WHY AM I SEEN *SO FREQUENTLY* IN THIS CHURCH WHEN I AM CLEARLY *NOT* A CHRISTIAN?

HOW MUCH MONEY WILL IT TAKE TO *BUY* YOUR CHURCH?

¡GASP!¿

MR. BURNS!

I'M AFRAID THIS CHURCH IS *NOT FOR SALE!*

OH, THAT'S A PITY. REMOVE THE MONEY, SMITHERS.

BACK IN THE LIMOUSINE, SIR?

NO, THAT'S TOO MUCH TROUBLE. JUST *BURN IT* IN THE PARKING LOT.

WAIT! WHILE THE CHURCH ISN'T *FOR SALE*...

...THERE'S NOTHING IN THE BIBLE AGAINST...

...*SPONSORSHIP!*

EXCELLENT!

GOOD LORD, ⸨CHOKE!⸩

SOON...

I DON'T THINK I LIKE THE IDEA OF MR. BURNS SPONSORING THE CHURCH.

OH, MARGE! EVERYTHING HAS A SPONSOR. THE *BIG OIL COMPANIES* SPONSOR THE *GOVERNMENT* AND THAT'S ⸨COUGH⸩ WORKED OUT ⸨HACK⸩ FINE!

EXODUS

HELLO, SIR. ARE YOU HAPPY WITH YOUR RELIGIOUS SERVICE?

NOT REALLY.

WOULD YOU CARE TO SWITCH TO *WICCA* FREE FOR A MONTH?

WICCA, EH?

WE'RE HAPPY WITH OUR RELIGION, THANK YOU!

REMEMBER WHEN YOU BECAME A *MONK* FOR TWO MONTHS AFTER TALKING TO THAT *BUDDHIST*? I'M NOT GOING THROUGH *THAT* AGAIN.

AS YOU CAN SEE, THE STAINED GLASS WINDOWS HAVE BEEN *CHANGED*. MR. BURNS TELLS ME THIS IS JUST *TEMPORARY* AND THE APOSTLES ARE *ON ORDER*.

HEY, LOOK! THERE ARE ONLY *FIVE* COMMANDMENTS NOW!

‡WHEW!‡ THAT'S *WAY EASIER* TO REMEMBER.

REVEREND, MAY I SAY A FEW WORDS?

WELL, I...

TAKE FIVE, PADRE!

AS YOU CAN SEE, I'VE MADE A *FEW CHANGES*, AND I THINK YOU'LL *ENJOY* THEM.

HEY, EACH PEW HAS A *MAKE YOUR OWN TACO BAR!*

NOW THAT'S *GOOD RELIGION!*

ONE SMALL THING. IT'S NOW A *SIN* TO BELONG TO THE *FOLLOWING ORGANIZATIONS*...

...THE ENVIRONMENTAL PROTECTION AGENCY, GREENPEACE, AND LISA SIMPSON'S TREE HUGGING SOCIETY.

WHAT? WHY I...

QUIET, *SINNER!* LEST YE DAMN US ALL!

I'M WARNING YOU...

SOON...

SO YOU NEED A *NEW* RELIGION, HUH?

I FEEL SO *EMPTY* INSIDE.

THEN, BROTHER, YOU CAME TO THE RIGHT PLACE. IT'S GREAT BEING JEWISH!

THE FOOD'S GOOD, AND THERE'S *MORE HOLIDAYS* THAN YOU CAN SHAKE A STICK AT.

COME WITH ME!

I LOVED THE MATZO BALL SOUP AND THE KNISHES, BUT THIS PRODUCTION OF "FIDDLER ON THE ROOF" IS A BIT *DEPRESSING*.

IT'S THE *ORTHODOX VERSION*. THE DAUGHTERS ALL *LISTEN* TO THEIR FATHER, TEVYE, INSTEAD OF *REBELLING*.

BUT THEY ALL DIE *OLD MAIDS*.

C'MON, LET'S GET OUT TO THE SNACK TABLE BEFORE ALL THE KUGEL'S GONE!

WELL DONE.

CLAP!

CLAP!

EXCELLENT!

CLAP!

CLAP!

I PARTICULARLY ENJOYED THE *LACK OF DANCING*.

CLAP!

YOUR LOSS.

I DON'T KNOW. I JUST DON'T THINK THE SHOE FITS ME.

BUT IF YOU CHANGE YOUR MIND, HERE'S A *COUPON* FOR A BUY-ONE-GET-ONE -FREE *BRIS*.

LATER...

THE LIFE OF A HINDU IS A *PEACEFUL* AND *FULFILLING* ONE!

WHAT? I CAN'T *HEAR* YOU OVER YOUR CRYING CHILDREN, THE CASH REGISTER, AND GUNFIRE!

WAAAAAH!

WAAAA'!

CH. CHING!

BANG!

BANG!

DUDE! I'M LIKE TOTALLY IN A *RUSH*.

I SAID THE LIFE OF A HINDU IS A *PEACEFUL* AND *FULFILLING* ONE!

!SIGH!

NO LOITERING!

POW!

Duff

OPEN

157

EVEN LATER...

YOU REALLY SHOULD CONSIDER *SNAKE HANDLING* AS YOUR NEW RELIGION!

HSSSSSSS

AAAAAH!

HEY, NED, BE A PAL AND *CALL 911*, WOULD YA?

MAN, THE ONLY DAY I DON'T BRING *MY KNIFE* TO WORK!

HSSSSSSSSSSSSSSSSS

LATER STILL...

I CAN OFFER YOU A RELIGION OF *BLISS* AND *CONTENTMENT*.

WELCOME TO KRUSTY BURGER

HEY, AM I PAYING YOU TO *CLEAN THE GREASE TRAPS* OR *RECRUIT* FOR YOUR CULT?

TO CLEAN THE TRAPS ...SIR!

WELCOME TO KRUSTY BURGER

:SIGH.:

OOOF!

AAAH! SORRY!

CRASH!

EASY THERE! WHAT'S THE SUN-DAY RUSH?

WE'RE *LATE* FOR CHURCH, AND THE MINISTER IS *AWFUL STRICT!*

STRICT YOU SAY?

IS THIS *OLD-TIME RELIGION?*

REALLY OLD, YEAH!

MIND IF I TAG ALONG?

AS LONG AS YOU DON'T MIND *LONG SERMONS* AND *HARD PEWS.*

THANK YOU, LORD!

MEANWHILE...

WILL *I* EVER GET TO TALK?

I DON'T KNOW. MR. BURNS IS REALLY *ENJOYING* THIS. HE EVEN BUYS HIS CLOTHES AT "THE HOUSE OF SHARPTON" NOW.

BROTHERS AND SISTERS. I HAVE A *PARABLE* FOR YOU!

LOOK AT THE VIDEO MONITOR IF YOU WILL.

THE MAN
WHO PLANTED
ATOMS

"ONCE UPON A TIME THERE WAS A MAN WHO PLANTED *ATOMS*."

"HE WOULD THROW THEM HITHER AND YON!"

"THE ATOMS THAT FELL ON THE *ROAD*..."

"...WELL, NOTHING HAPPENED."

"THE ONES THAT FELL ON *RICH SOIL*..."

"...THE SAME. NOTHING! ZIP! NADA!"

"BUT THE ATOMS THAT FELL IN A *WELL-MAINTAINED NUCLEAR FACILITY* SUPPLIED *CLEAN, EFFICIENT ENERGY* FOR *EVERYONE!*"

I'M CONFUSED.

YOU'RE SAYING OUR *SOULS* ARE LIKE ATOMS?

NO! NO! NO! NUCLEAR ENERGY IS THE *SOUL* OF *THIS TOWN!*

IT WAS A *SUBTLE ALLEGORY*. IF YOU NEED ME TO BE AS HAM-FISTED AS C.S. LEWIS, I WILL BE!

LATER...

MR. BURNS, I'M AFRAID THIS JUST ISN'T WORKING OUT.

I AGREE.

YOU DO? WELL, THAT'S A RELIEF. YOU SEE...

YOU'RE *FIRED!*

WHAT?!!

BUT YOU *CAN'T* FIRE ME!

I'VE PAID TO *RENOVATE* THE ENTIRE CHURCH IN THE LAST TWO WEEKS. THERE'S NOT AN *ORIGINAL* BRICK OR BOARD OF WOOD LEFT. I *OWN* THIS BUILDING. PLUS I'M BRINGING *THE CROWDS* IN!

YOU ARE *THE WEAKEST LINK. GOODBYE.*

I DON'T GET THAT AT ALL.

IT'S A LINE FROM A POPULAR TELEVISION PROGRAM.

I DON'T WATCH TV.

NOT EVEN *PBS?*

WELL, YES...PBS.

THEN YOU WATCH TV. I *HATE* WHEN PEOPLE SAY THAT!

OH, JUST *GET OUT!*

MEANWHILE...

WELL BOYS, HOW ARE YOU ENJOYING THE SERVICE?

I DON'T KNOW DADDY. SOMETHING SEEMS *WRONG.*

I MISS OUR OLD CHURCH.

I DO TOO, TODD, BUT THIS IS THE *NEXT BEST THING*.

WHY DOES HE HAVE A *GOAT'S HEAD* ON HIS CHEST?

GOATS ARE GOD'S CREATURES TOO, SON.

YOU CAN'T WARN FOLKS TOO MUCH ABOUT HIM! WE MUST ALWAYS *BE ON GUARD*.

HE SURE TALKS ABOUT *THE DEVIL* A LOT.

LATER...

HEY, LISA, WANT TO GET SOME *ICE CREAM*? MY TREAT.

BART, WHERE DID YOU GET THE MONEY?

REVEREND LOVEJOY'S *THREE CARD MONTE* GAME.

REVEREND LOVEJOY! WHAT ARE YOU DOING?

LOSING MY SHIRT.

I'M BROKE, AND I HEARD THAT THIS WAS SUPPOSED TO BE A *SURE-FIRE MONEYMAKER*.

ARE YOU *CHEATING*?

OF COURSE NOT. THAT WOULD BE *WRONG*!

LATER...

WE NEED YOU BACK AT THE CHURCH, REVEREND.

BUT EVERYONE ENJOYS MR. BURNS' SERMONS WITH HIS *INFOMERCIAL CARTOONS*.

THEY'RE GETTING *BORING* NOW.

COMMERCIALS ARE FUN *THE FIRST TIME*, BUT THEY GET OLD REALLY FAST.

CAN YOU HELP ME GET MY JOB BACK?

I'M GLAD YOU ASKED! WE HAVE A PLAN!

THAT NIGHT, OUTSIDE THE SPRINGFIELD COMMUNITY CHURCH...

I'VE GOT A *BAD* FEELING ABOUT THIS, CHILDREN...

164

IT'S THE **SAME BIBLE**.

YES.

THE **SAME SAVIOR**?

YES.

BUT **NO POPE**?

NO.

SMITHERS WE'RE **LEAVING**. THIS RELIGION BUSINESS IS **MORE CONFUSING** THAN **THE INTERNET**.

YAY!

BUT FIRST, BEFORE I GIVE THE CHURCH BACK TO YOU, I'D LIKE YOU TO **INDULGE ME**.

CERTAINLY, WHAT CAN I DO?

AS I SAID. INDULGE ME. IN EXCHANGE FOR THE CHURCH BACK YOU'LL GIVE ME AN **INDULGENCE**.

YOU MEAN **BUY** YOUR WAY INTO **HEAVEN**? BUT THE CHURCH HASN'T DONE THAT IN **YEARS**.

IT'S STILL WITHIN YOUR **JURISDICTION**. I'VE MADE A **FEW ERRORS** IN MY TIME AND I NEED A **GUARANTEE** I'LL GET INTO HEAVEN WHEN I DIE.

JUST WRITE IT DOWN AND THE CHURCH IS **YOURS**.

EXCELLENT!

I'LL LEAVE A **COPY** FOR YOUR FILES AND BID YOU GOOD NIGHT!

OH MY SWEET LORD! IS THIS REALLY A CHURCH OF SATAN?

OF COURSE, IT IS! IT'S *WRITTEN* ON ALL OUR *STATIONERY*.

RUN BOYS, RUN!

WELL, WE *SCARED* ANOTHER ONE OFF. IS IT *ME*?

DON'T BEAT YOURSELF UP, ROY.

WHO WANTS TO MAKE *TOLL HOUSE COOKIES*?

AW! YOU GUYS ARE *THE BEST*!

LATER...

WELCOME BACK TO THE FLOCK, NED.

THANKS, REVEREND. IT FEELS LIKE *HOME*! ARE THE TACO BARS STILL HERE?

NO, BUT NOW IF EVERY-ONE PAYS ATTENTION, I SPRING FOR *PIZZA* AFTERWARDS.

WHAT ARE *YOU* DOING HERE?

I HEARD THERE WAS PIZZA.

A *FREE MEAL* IS A FREE MEAL.

HOW MARGE GOT HER CURTAINS BACK

ARGH! HOMER! QUICK! PULL THEM *OUT!*

MARGE, I'M *TRYING,* BUT IT WON'T LET GO!

STUPID *GARBAGE DISPOSAL!* STUPID *CURTAINS!* D'OH!

RRRIIIIP!

MY CURTAINS ARE *NOT* STUPID! I MADE THEM *MYSELF,* AND NOW THEY'RE *RUINED!*

NOW I NEED TO SEW *NEW* ONES...

NOW, MARGE, IF *HISTORY* HAS TAUGHT US ANYTHING, IT'S THAT HANGING CURTAINS NEAR THE GARBAGE DISPOSAL LEADS TO *NOTHING* BUT *TROUBLE!*

MIGHT I RECOMMEND A NICE *TIN-FOIL* WINDOW COVERING?

'ESSE McCANN AND ABBY DENSON
STORY

PHIL ORTIZ
PENCILS

PHYLLIS NOVIN
INKS

ART VILLANUEVA
COLORS

KAREN BATES
LETTERS

MATT GROENING
INTERIOR DECORATOR

OGDENVILLE...

HRMMM. *CLOSE* BUT NO CIGAR.

OGDENVILLE! *HAH!* THE PEOPLE HERE ARE SO *FULL* OF THEMSELVES! OOOH! I'M FROM OGDENVILLE! I AM *SOOO* SPECIAL!

OH, DEAR! PLEASE *EXCUSE* ME.

UUUH!

BUMP!

SEE WHAT I MEAN! THE PEOPLE HERE ARE *SO RUDE* WITH THEIR *HIGH* AND *MIGHTY OGDENVILLEAN ATTITUDES!*

OH, HUSH. WE WON'T BE HERE MUCH *LONGER!*

MAY I *HELP* YOU MISS?

YES. WE'RE LOOKING FOR FABRIC WITH A *CORNCOB* PATTERN.

COULD YOU PLEASE *WAIT* HERE A MOMENT? I'LL BE RIGHT BACK.

ANOTHER *"CONTACT"* IS HERE. SHE KNEW THE *CODE WORD:* "CORNCOB".

VERY GOOD. PROCEED WITH *PHASE TWO.*

YOUR *INSTRUCTIONS* ARE IN THIS ENVELOPE. IT CONTAINS ALL THE *INFORMA-TION* YOU NEED. YOU MUST *DESTROY* IT *IMMEDIATELY* AFTER READING IT.

OH, *MY!* CORN-COB FABRIC MUST BE GETTING *VERY* POPULAR!

THE END